THE 10

Most Decisive Battles On American Soil

R. B. Hallett

Series Editor
Jeffrey D. Wilhelm

Much thought, debate, and research went into choosing and ranking the 10 items in each book in this series. We realize that everyone has his or her own opinion of what is most significant, revolutionary, amazing, deadly, and so on. As you read, you may agree with our choices, or you may be surprised — and that's the way it should be!

Franklin Watts®
an imprint of
SCHOLASTIC
www.scholastic.com/librarypublishing

A Rubicon book published in association with Scholastic Inc.

Rubicon © 2008 Rubicon Publishing Inc.
www.rubiconpublishing.com

All rights reserved. No part of this publication may be reproduced, stored in a database or retrieval system, distributed, or transmitted in any form or by any means, electronic, mechanical, photocopying, recording, or otherwise, without the prior written permission of Rubicon Publishing Inc.

THE 10 is a trademark of The 10 Books

SCHOLASTIC and associated logos and designs are trademarks and/or registered trademarks of Scholastic Inc.

Associate Publishers: Kim Koh, Miriam Bardswich
Project Editor: Amy Land
Editor: Bettina Iozzo
Creative Director: Jennifer Drew
Project Manager/Designer: Jeanette MacLean
Graphic Designer: Julie Whatman

The publisher gratefully acknowledges the following for permission to reprint copyrighted material in this book.

Every reasonable effort has been made to trace the owners of copyrighted material and to make due acknowledgment. Any errors or omissions drawn to our attention will be gladly rectified in future editions.

"Revenge for Texas," excerpt of a personal account by Creed Taylor.
From Sons of DeWitt Colony Texas.

Cover image: Battle of New Orleans–Library of Congress/LC-USZC4-6878

Library and Archives Canada Cataloguing in Publication

Hallett, R. B.
   The 10 most decisive battles on American soil / Robert Hallett.

ISBN 978-1-55448-538-3

   1. Readers (Elementary). 2. Readers—Battles—United States.
I. Title. II. Title: Ten most decisive battles on American soil.

PE1117.H346 2007   428.6   C2007-906883-9

1 2 3 4 5 6 7 8 9 10   10   17 16 15 14 13 12 11 10 09 08
Printed in Singapore

Contents

Introduction: The Road to Freedom 4

Battle of the Aleutian Islands 6
It seemed as though the Japanese army was well-entrenched on these islands. Was this true?

Battle of Lake Erie 10
The U.S. had to win this battle to protect Ohio, Pennsylvania, and western New York from a land invasion.

Battle of the Little Bighorn 14
This was a decisive but short-lived victory for the Cheyenne and Sioux tribes.

Battle of San Jacinto 18
Texas became the Lone Star Republic as a result of this conflict.

Battle of New Orleans 22
This battle was fought two weeks after the War of 1812 had ended!

Battle of Lexington and Concord 26
No one knows who fired the "shot heard 'round the world," but it began a revolution.

Battle of Trenton 30
Christmas didn't stop the Continental Army from fighting this battle.

Battle of Pearl Harbor 34
This tragic day led to the United States' declaration of war in World War II.

Battle of Yorktown 38
American forces and their French allies joined up to defeat the British in this last great battle of the Revolutionary War.

Battle of Gettysburg 42
Both sides suffered heavy losses in this deadly Civil War battle.

We Thought 46

What Do You Think? 47

Index 48

THE ROAD TO FREEDOM

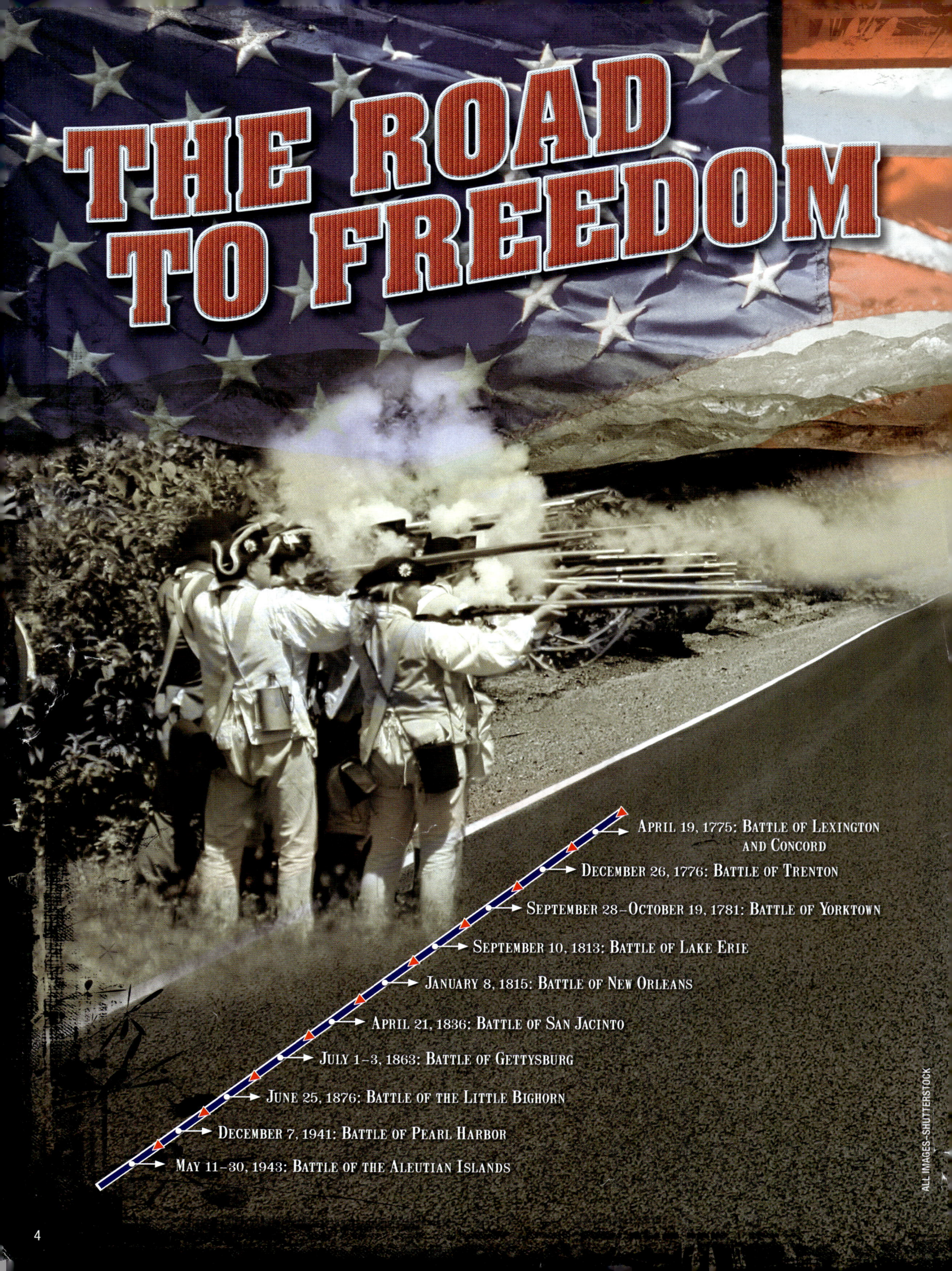

- April 19, 1775: Battle of Lexington and Concord
- December 26, 1776: Battle of Trenton
- September 28–October 19, 1781: Battle of Yorktown
- September 10, 1813: Battle of Lake Erie
- January 8, 1815: Battle of New Orleans
- April 21, 1836: Battle of San Jacinto
- July 1–3, 1863: Battle of Gettysburg
- June 25, 1876: Battle of the Little Bighorn
- December 7, 1941: Battle of Pearl Harbor
- May 11–30, 1943: Battle of the Aleutian Islands

What does freedom mean to you? What does it mean for your country?

Freedom was one of the motivations for the creation of the United States of America in 1776. And in order to protect their freedom and territory, Americans have engaged in many battles and wars during their short history. After the Revolutionary War against the mighty British Empire, Americans went on to wage battles with other foreign nations and different groups of Americans. It was a history of struggles and bloodshed, and, at times, misguided decisions. But it was also a history of courage and determination.

In this book, we invite you to relive what we think were the 10 most decisive battles fought on American soil. You will notice that the battles do not appear in the order in which they took place in history, as they do in the timeline on page 4. Instead, they are presented according to how we have ranked them, from least to most decisive, based on these criteria: the extent to which the battle influenced the outcome of its war; the importance of the battle's impact on the nation; the number of lives lost in the battle; and the rights and freedoms won or lost as a result of the battle.

Join us on the battleground and think like a historian when answering this question:

WHICH WAS THE MOST DECISIVE BATTLE ON U.S. SOIL?

10 BATTLE OF THE

Soldiers pour from their landing boats onto the beach at Massacre Bay, Attu Island.

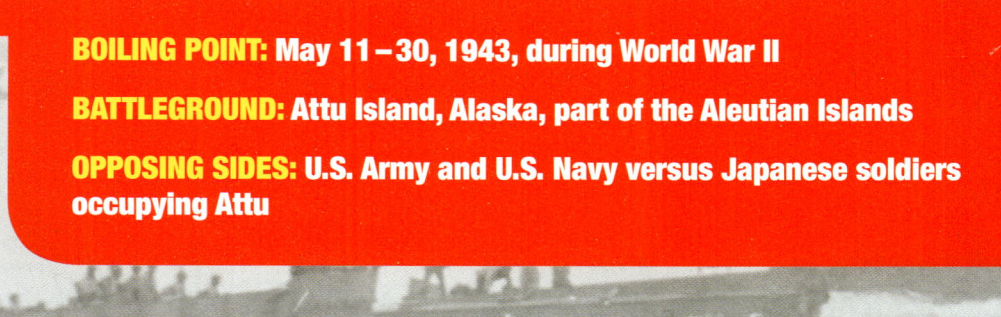

ALEUTIAN ISLANDS

BOILING POINT: May 11–30, 1943, during World War II

BATTLEGROUND: Attu Island, Alaska, part of the Aleutian Islands

OPPOSING SIDES: U.S. Army and U.S. Navy versus Japanese soldiers occupying Attu

The Aleutian Islands are a chain of islands that belong to the United States. They are located in the Pacific Ocean, about 1,100 to 1,200 miles from the Alaskan mainland. In June 1942, during World War II, Japanese troops invaded three of the islands — Adak, Attu, and Kiska. Many historians consider this invasion to have been an attempt to divert American forces away from the main Japanese attack at Midway Atoll in the North Pacific Ocean.

On August 30, American soldiers retook Adak. The other two islands would remain in Japanese hands for almost a year. Just two weeks after taking Adak, army engineers had built an airfield on the island. From there, the U.S. began air attacks on Kiska. The Japanese then sent reinforcements to both Kiska and Attu. The Americans continued their attacks. In March 1943, U.S. ships set up a naval blockade around the Japanese-occupied islands.

In May, American troops prepared for an invasion of the islands. Although Kiska was the more important military target, the U.S. decided to head to Attu first. There were fewer Japanese soldiers occupying the smaller island. On May 11, 1943, American forces landed on Attu. Nineteen days later, they won a resounding victory.

---

naval blockade: *measure that used warships to prevent troops and supplies from reaching the enemy*

BATTLE OF THE ALEUTIAN ISLANDS

THE BATTLE BEGINS

U.S. soldiers planned to invade the island of Attu at the end of April. Because of bad weather, they postponed their invasion until May 11, when two U.S. Army forces landed on the island. The Northern Force had little difficulty landing and took no casualties. However, the Southern Force met heavy Japanese gunfire as it advanced through Massacre Valley in clear weather. The U.S. soldiers had a difficult time locating the Japanese soldiers, who were hidden on the ridges where the fog was very heavy. They were the first to suffer casualties.

THE TURNING POINT

By May 28, U.S. troops had surrounded the Japanese near Chichagof Harbor. They planned to attack the next morning, but the Japanese had a surprise for them. Early in the morning, they charged the American lines. Screaming and waving swords and bayonets, hundreds of Japanese soldiers ran out of the darkness. U.S. troops were caught off guard. But after terrible hand-to-hand fighting, the Americans won the battle.

casualties: *wounded or dead*

American soldiers launch mortar shells on Attu.

IN THE END

The Japanese lost more than 2,600 soldiers in the battle. Only 28 survived to be taken prisoner. By May 30, Attu was back in American hands. The U.S. lost 549 soldiers and around 1,150 men suffered injuries. Their next target was the island of Kiska. American and Canadian forces landed on the island in mid-August — only to find it vacant!

? Why do you think the Japanese abandoned Kiska?

? Why do you think the Japanese tried a surprise attack? Do you think swords and bayonets could ever defeat troops armed with guns? Explain your answers.

Quick Fact

U.S. soldiers were ill-prepared for the extremely cold weather on Attu. In addition to those injured in battle, another 2,100 Americans suffered non-battle injuries such as trench foot. This is an ailment caused by cold, wet, and unclean conditions such as those suffered by soldiers in the trenches during World War I. A soldier with trench foot will have his foot amputated if it is not treated in time.

The Expert Says...

"In clearing the Japanese invaders from the Aleutians, the objective had been partly to eliminate a potential military threat but mainly to eradicate a psychological blot. Japan's foothold in the Western Hemisphere was gone."

— George L. MacGarrigle, U.S. Army Center of Military History

eradicate: *erase; do away with*

Every Citizen a Soldier in World War II

Why were war posters so important? Check out the poster to the right and read the explanation below.

At the beginning of World War II, the United States tried to stay out of the war. It was being fought in Asia and Europe, far from the U.S. Things changed when two battles took place on American soil. First, the Japanese attacked Pearl Harbor in Hawaii. Six months later, they invaded the Aleutian Islands.

The U.S. was now at war! Posters were created to encourage Americans to do their part on the home front, building war machines and manufacturing ammunition. The poster to the right is a reminder to Americans that, if they did not help the effort on the home front, war could still come to American soil.

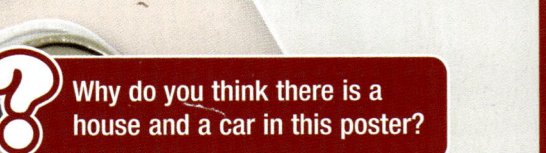

? Why do you think there is a house and a car in this poster?

Take Note

The Battle of the Aleutian Islands comes in at #10 on our list. It was one of two major World War II battles fought on American soil. The victory was a morale booster as the Aleutian Islands were the first lost American territory to be reclaimed.
- Why were posters effective in encouraging Americans to help with the war effort during World War II? Would they still be as effective today? Why or why not?

9 BATTLE OF LA

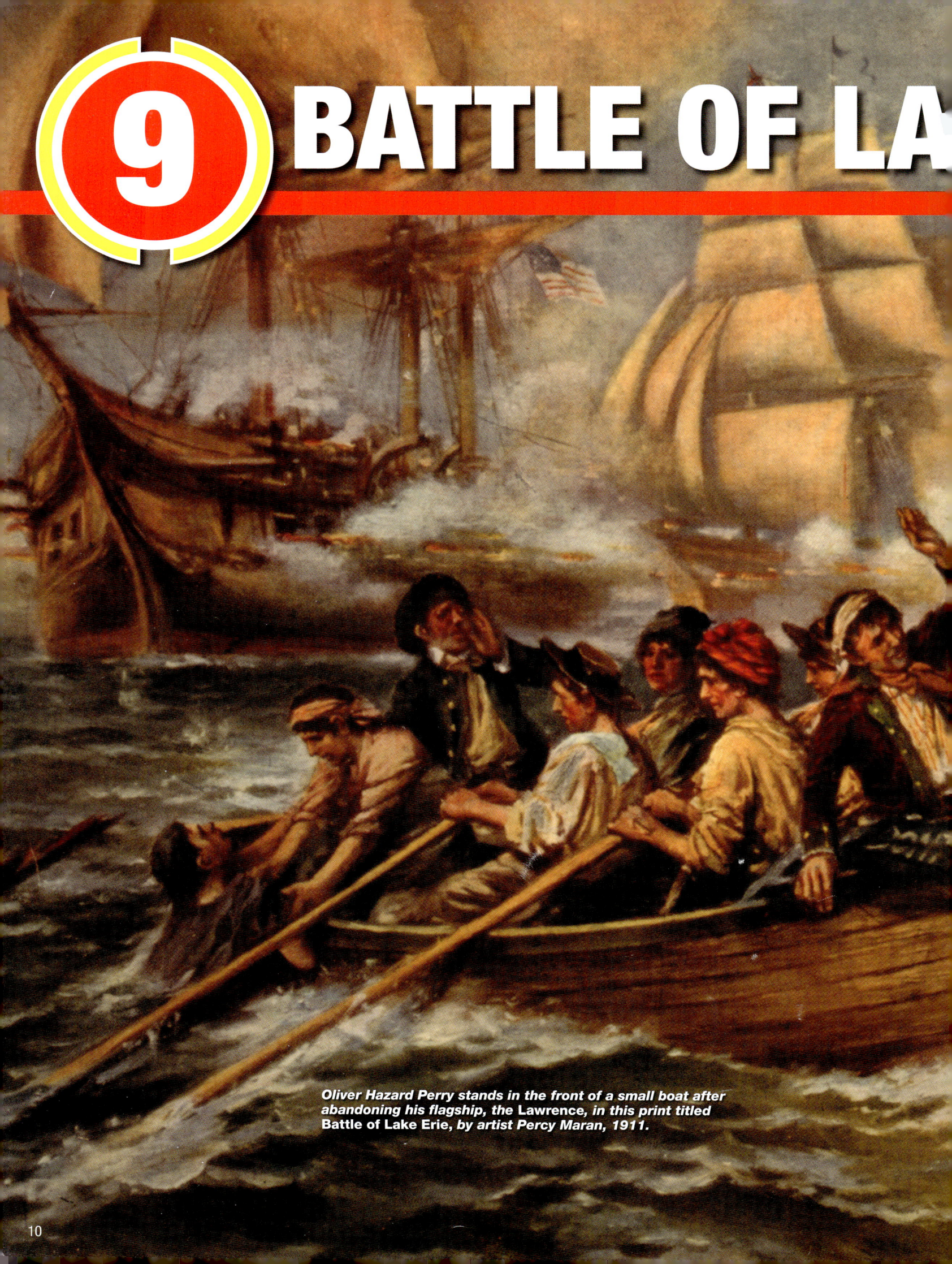

Oliver Hazard Perry stands in the front of a small boat after abandoning his flagship, the Lawrence, in this print titled Battle of Lake Erie, by artist Percy Maran, 1911.

KE ERIE

BOILING POINT: September 10, 1813
BATTLEGROUND: Lake Erie, off the coast of Ohio
OPPOSING SIDES: British navy versus American navy

The War of 1812 was part of a larger war between Britain and France that began in 1803. The U.S. became involved when Britain began to interfere in American affairs such as foreign trade and shipping. One major concern was the British practice of impressment, or kidnapping American sailors to work on British ships. In June, British sailors opened fire on the U.S. *Chesapeake* after they were refused permission to board the ship. Three U.S. sailors were killed and 18 were wounded.

Americans were also angry about Britain's interference in the Northwest. Britain was arming Native Americans, who were using the weapons to fight against U.S. settlers.

In 1812, the U.S. declared war on Britain. At first, the U.S. had many victories at sea. Then the British blockaded the coast, preventing American ships and supplies from leaving and entering ports along the Atlantic Ocean. But the most important naval battle took place on Lake Erie. The British needed to control the lake so they could ship troops and supplies from Canada to Ohio, Pennsylvania, and New York.

The Battle of Lake Erie lasted only a few hours, but it secured control of the lake for the U.S. It was a monumental victory for the Americans against a much more powerful and experienced opponent.

BATTLE OF LAKE ERIE

THE BATTLE BEGINS

In the summer of 1813, British and American naval forces played a waiting game on Lake Erie. The American commander, Oliver Perry, spent the summer avoiding the British navy while his troops built more ships. At the same time, the British were waiting for supplies to arrive from their stronghold at Montreal, Quebec, hundreds of miles to the northeast. Perry knew that if the British kept control of Lake Erie, they could bring troops across the lake from Canada whenever they wanted. In August, Perry moved his forces to Put-in-Bay on South Bass Island, Ohio, and waited for the British.

Quick Fact
The *Lawrence* sailed into battle flying a banner that read, "Don't give up the ship."

THE TURNING POINT

Early in the morning on September 10, American guards spotted British ships sailing toward South Bass Island. Perry's ship, the *Lawrence*, sailed into battle first. Although it inflicted heavy damage on the British, the *Lawrence* was a wreck. Its guns were knocked out and four-fifths of its sailors were dead or wounded. Just when it looked as if he would have to surrender, Perry escaped in a rowboat to the *Niagara*. The wind had shifted and was now much stronger. The small American gunboats that had been separated from the *Lawrence* were now able to catch up to the *Niagara*. Perry sailed close to the British ships, helped by the stronger wind, and opened fire. When the small U.S. gunboats joined in, the British captain Robert Barclay realized his fleet was no match for the Americans. One by one, the British ships surrendered.

? Perry accepted Barclay's surrender on the heavily-damaged *Lawrence* instead of the *Niagara*. Why do you think this was?

Enlarged map of the battle location

IN THE END

Perry's small force had won a massive victory. Barclay sent one of his officers to officially surrender to Perry and hand over his sword. The surrender took place on the deck of the damaged *Lawrence*. Perry then sent a note to his commander, General William Harrison. The note said, "We have met the enemy, and they are ours." A month after the Battle of Lake Erie, General Harrison defeated the British at the Battle of the Thames in what is now Ontario, Canada. Ohio, Pennsylvania, and western New York were now safe for the rest of the war.

Quick Fact
The Battle of the Thames claimed the life of Tecumseh, a famous Native-American warrior and ally of the British.

The Expert Says...
" The complete defeat of Barclay's squadron immediately changed the military situation on the Western frontier. ... With the end of the War of 1812, the Great Lakes never again saw naval warfare. "
— Eric G. Swedin, contributor to *Military History* magazine

Military Life in 1812

Life was hard for everyone 200 years ago, but few had it as tough as soldiers and sailors. Read this list of facts about military life during the War of 1812.

★ Soldiers and sailors in the War of 1812 often wore their own clothes. But others were given a coat, one or two pairs of pants, and maybe two or three shirts during their time in the military. It was often one size fits all. So if things didn't fit, it was their problem!

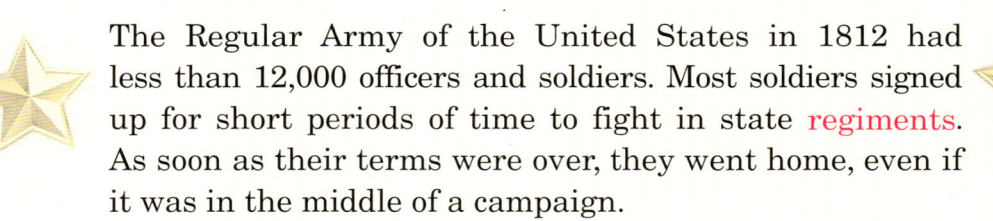

★ The Regular Army of the United States in 1812 had less than 12,000 officers and soldiers. Most soldiers signed up for short periods of time to fight in state regiments. As soon as their terms were over, they went home, even if it was in the middle of a campaign.

regiments: *military units of about 600 soldiers*

★ Food (if there was any) was always pretty boring. Soldiers generally received pickled meat and either flour or dried peas. They boiled this together into a thick sludge. They often ate this day after day.

★ Soldiers and sailors could be very young. Twelve-year-old boys were recruited to be drummers and cabin boys, while many other soldiers and sailors were barely teenagers.

? Today Americans have to be 18 years old before they can enter the military. Do you agree with this age requirement? How old should Americans be before they join the military? Explain your answer.

Take Note

The Battle of Lake Erie sails into the #9 spot. The Battle of the Aleutian Islands was a major victory for the Americans, but the U.S. was already a powerful nation. Britain was considered stronger than the U.S. during the War of 1812, but the victory on Lake Erie proved that the U.S. would not be defeated easily.
- It took two wars (Revolutionary War and War of 1812) for Britain to realize that the United States could not be dominated anymore. Why do you think it was so hard for Britain to accept this?

5   4   3   2   1

8 BATTLE OF THE

The Custer Fight, a painting by Charles M. Russell from 1903, shows Native Americans charging into battle at the Little Bighorn.

LITTLE BIGHORN

BOILING POINT: June 25, 1876

BATTLEGROUND: Little Bighorn River, eastern Montana Territory

OPPOSING SIDES: Sioux and Cheyenne tribes versus the U.S. Cavalry

The Battle of the Little Bighorn, also known as "Custer's Last Stand," is probably the best-known conflict between the U.S. military and Native Americans. And it was a decisive victory for the Plains tribes.

Conflict began with discoveries of gold in the Black Hills of what is now South Dakota, in the 1860s and 70s. In 1868, the Sioux, Cheyenne, and Arapaho tribes had signed a treaty with U.S. officials. This treaty gave the tribes reservations in the Black Hills region. But prospectors looking for gold ignored the treaty and entered the reservations. In the winter of 1875-6, many thousands of Sioux and Cheyenne warriors, under the command of Crazy Horse and Sitting Bull, left their reservations and banded together to push back the trespassers. The Seventh Cavalry, led by Lieutenant Colonel George A. Custer, was sent to return the Native Americans to their reservations.

What Custer didn't realize was that he and his troops were greatly outnumbered. The Battle of the Little Bighorn would be a decisive victory for the Sioux and Cheyenne.

---

reservations: *areas of land set aside for Native Americans to live on*

prospectors: *people who explore a region in search of valuable minerals, such as gold*

BATTLE OF THE LITTLE BIGHORN

Quick Fact
At the Battle of the Little Bighorn, Crazy Horse (Tasunko Witko) was a war leader and an organizer of the battle. Sitting Bull (Tatanka Iyotaka) did not take part in the fighting. He was a spiritual leader.

THE BATTLE BEGINS
On the morning of June 25, 1876, Custer divided his 600 troops into three groups, keeping one group under his own command. The second group, under the command of Captain Frederick Benteen, traveled to the southwest, 10 miles away from the Little Bighorn River. The third group, under Major Marcus Reno, was sent to the other side of the river. The route that Custer and his troops took is unclear, but it seems that the battle began when they spotted a small group of Native-American warriors. Without alerting Benteen and Reno of his plan to attack, Custer led a charge against the Native Americans, not realizing that these warriors were actually just a few among thousands.

THE TURNING POINT
It's difficult to know exactly what happened, but it appears that Custer's small force was caught in a pincer movement by the Sioux and Cheyenne. In less than two hours, Custer and all of his 210 men were dead.

IN THE END
At first, this appeared to be a major victory for the Native-American tribes. But it didn't take long for the U.S. government to send more troops to force the Sioux and Cheyenne back to their reservations. In 1877, Crazy Horse surrendered to U.S. forces. Sitting Bull and his followers fled to Canada, but returned to the U.S. and surrendered in 1881. The Sioux and Cheyenne returned to their reservations where the boundary lines were redrawn. The Black Hills were now outside reservation land and open to prospectors. In 1922, Sioux tribes filed a lawsuit against the U.S. government for compensation. To this day, ownership of the Black Hills has not been settled.

pincer movement: *two-headed attack against both sides of an enemy force, intended to surround and crush an enemy as if in a claw*

? Do you agree with the boundary lines being moved to meet the desires of the prospectors? Explain.

A reproduction of a painting by Frederic Remington depicting Custer's Last Stand

Quick Fact
It is estimated that the total number of Native-American warriors who died at the hands of Custer's men is between 30 and 50.

The Expert Says...
"Much has been said and written about the Battle of the Little Bighorn River, but our histories of this conflict largely exclude perspectives of the native victors."

— Richard A. Fox, professor of anthropology at the University of South Dakota

perspectives: *points of view*

Two Sides to a Story

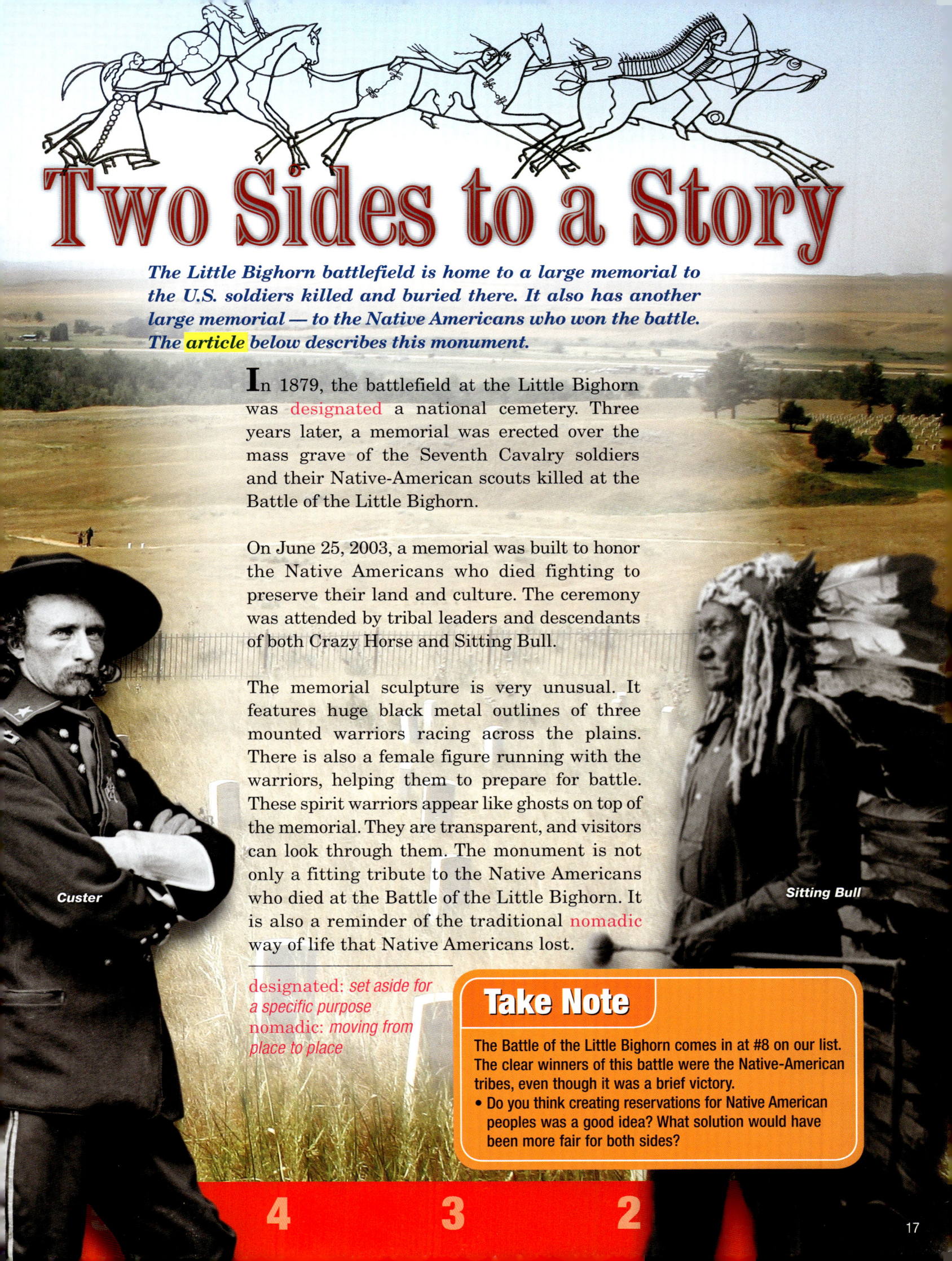

The Little Bighorn battlefield is home to a large memorial to the U.S. soldiers killed and buried there. It also has another large memorial — to the Native Americans who won the battle. The article below describes this monument.

In 1879, the battlefield at the Little Bighorn was designated a national cemetery. Three years later, a memorial was erected over the mass grave of the Seventh Cavalry soldiers and their Native-American scouts killed at the Battle of the Little Bighorn.

On June 25, 2003, a memorial was built to honor the Native Americans who died fighting to preserve their land and culture. The ceremony was attended by tribal leaders and descendants of both Crazy Horse and Sitting Bull.

The memorial sculpture is very unusual. It features huge black metal outlines of three mounted warriors racing across the plains. There is also a female figure running with the warriors, helping them to prepare for battle. These spirit warriors appear like ghosts on top of the memorial. They are transparent, and visitors can look through them. The monument is not only a fitting tribute to the Native Americans who died at the Battle of the Little Bighorn. It is also a reminder of the traditional nomadic way of life that Native Americans lost.

Custer

Sitting Bull

designated: *set aside for a specific purpose*
nomadic: *moving from place to place*

Take Note

The Battle of the Little Bighorn comes in at #8 on our list. The clear winners of this battle were the Native-American tribes, even though it was a brief victory.
- Do you think creating reservations for Native American peoples was a good idea? What solution would have been more fair for both sides?

7 BATTLE OF SAN

Santa Anna Being Presented to Sam Houston by Norman Price; in this scene, captive Santa Anna (seated) is brought before General Sam Houston on April 22, 1836, the day after the Texian victory at San Jacinto.

JACINTO

BOILING POINT: April 21, 1836

BATTLEGROUND: San Jacinto River in southeastern Texas

OPPOSING SIDES: Texas revolutionaries versus Mexican army

It's easy to think that the map of the United States has always looked the same as it does today. However, 170 years ago, the map looked very different to U.S. citizens. The west coast had hardly been explored. Huge parts of the Southwest belonged to Mexico.

Texas was once part of Mexico. It was opened up to immigrants from the United States in the 1820s. But in 1830, Mexico passed a law halting immigration to Texas from the United States. It also forbade importing enslaved Africans and threatened to abolish slavery in the state. In 1833, General Antonio López de Santa Anna was elected president of Mexico. Within a year, he replaced all of the elected officials of the Mexican government with his own supporters. Several Mexican states, including Texas, were outraged. Texians rose in revolt the following year, in what became known as the Texas Revolution.

That fall, Santa Anna sent forces into Texas to put down the rebellion. On March 6, 1836, a small force of Texians were massacred at the Alamo mission. Shortly after, Santa Anna's army defeated Texian forces near Goliad (Goh-lee-ad) and executed almost 350 prisoners. On April 21, a Texian force took a much larger Mexican force by surprise near the San Jacinto (San Juh-sin-toh) River. In just 18 minutes, Santa Anna's Mexican soldiers were routed. Texas would become independent!

Texians: *English-speaking residents of the Mexican state of Texas*
mission: *religious center*
routed: *decisively defeated*

? Do some research. Find out what happened at the Alamo and at Goliad. Why do you think the Texians were not successful at those two battles?

BATTLE OF SAN JACINTO

THE BATTLE BEGINS

The Texians were under the command of General Sam Houston. The Mexican army was made up of about 1,500 well-trained veterans. Houston's army was about half that number and most of his men were settlers who did not have military training. Santa Anna was very confident. He considered Houston's army a mob, and as far as he could see, he had them trapped against the San Jacinto River. How wrong could he be?

? Does being well trained guarantee a better army? What other factors are important?

THE TURNING POINT

On the morning of April 21, Houston ordered the burning of the bridge over the San Jacinto River, cutting off the retreat for both armies. At 3:30 in the afternoon, the Texians advanced. General Santa Anna and his men were having their *siesta* and no lookouts had been posted. The Texians tore through the Mexican camp shouting, "Remember the Alamo!" and "Remember Goliad!" In less than 20 minutes, more than 600 Mexican troops had been killed. More than 200 were wounded and 700 were taken prisoner. The Texians lost only a handful of soldiers. General Santa Anna was captured the next day, when he was found hiding disguised as a common soldier.

siesta: Spanish word for a traditional afternoon nap

? What do you think was the main reason for the Texian success?

Map legend:
- Texian Victory April 1836
- Mexican Victory March 1836
- Territory later ceded by Mexico in 1848, after the Mexican-American War

IN THE END

Santa Anna was forced to sign a treaty recognizing the independence of Texas. An independent republic, nicknamed the Lone Star Republic after the single star on its flag, was set up. Sam Houston was elected president by a landslide. Texas remained independent until it joined the United States in 1845. However, Mexico still claimed Texas and the U.S. *annexation* of Texas led to war between the two countries in 1845. In 1848, at the end of the Mexican-American War, Mexico *ceded* Texas to the United States.

annexation: formal act of adding territory
ceded: transferred by treaty

The Expert Says...

" In the space of 18 minutes, Mexico had lost [a large] area of land … and events were put into motion that within 12 years would cost Mexico one-third of its *sovereign* territory. … Seldom in all of military history has more been accomplished in less time. "

— Allen Lee Hamilton, author of *100 Decisive Battles: From Ancient Times to the Present*

sovereign: independent

Revenge for Texas

Creed Taylor was just 16 years old when he joined the Texas **militia**. In this personal account, he describes what took place at the Battle of San Jacinto.

"... From the moment we set up our yell and opened fire there was **consternation** in the Mexican camp. The enemy was completely surprised. Most of the officers were asleep as some of them were found shot while they **reposed** on their cots, and it was apparent that the Mexican soldiers were just preparing their evening meal, as their tables were left spread when the assault came. It was about four o'clock and to add to their confusion the western sun was shining directly in the enemy's face. General Houston said he purposely had timed the attack so the sun would be in the Mexicans' eyes. The Mexicans were not cowards and for a time fought desperately. However, as the **onslaught** increased and the Texans became more desperate, the foe lost spirit and fell back, finally running toward the center of their encampment where their brave officers tried to rally them to their **colors**. But the rush was too fast for the Mexicans to escape the fury of the "diablos tejanos" (Texas Devils). Our men were avenging the death of their friends in the Alamo and at Goliad, and everyone was determined to take full toll. ..."

militia: armed forces called only in emergencies
consternation: alarm; concern
reposed: rested
onslaught: attack
colors: military flags or banners

Portrait of General Sam Houston

? Mexican officers were shot as they slept or rested. Many people would consider this an **atrocity**. What else could the attackers have done?

atrocity: *something brutal, wicked*

The San Jacinto Monument is located in Harris County, Texas, and is dedicated "to Heroes of the Battle of San Jacinto and all others who contributed to the independence of Texas." It's topped with a 220-ton star symbolizing the star on the flag of the Lone Star Republic.

Take Note

The Battle of San Jacinto ranks #7 on our list. This battle was a decisive victory for the Texians. It changed the course of American history, leading to the independence of Texas and, almost ten years later, the U.S. annexation of the state.
- Compare this battle with the Battle of the Little Bighorn. What are the similarities and differences? What do you think helped each winning side to come out on top?

3   2   1

6 BATTLE OF NEW

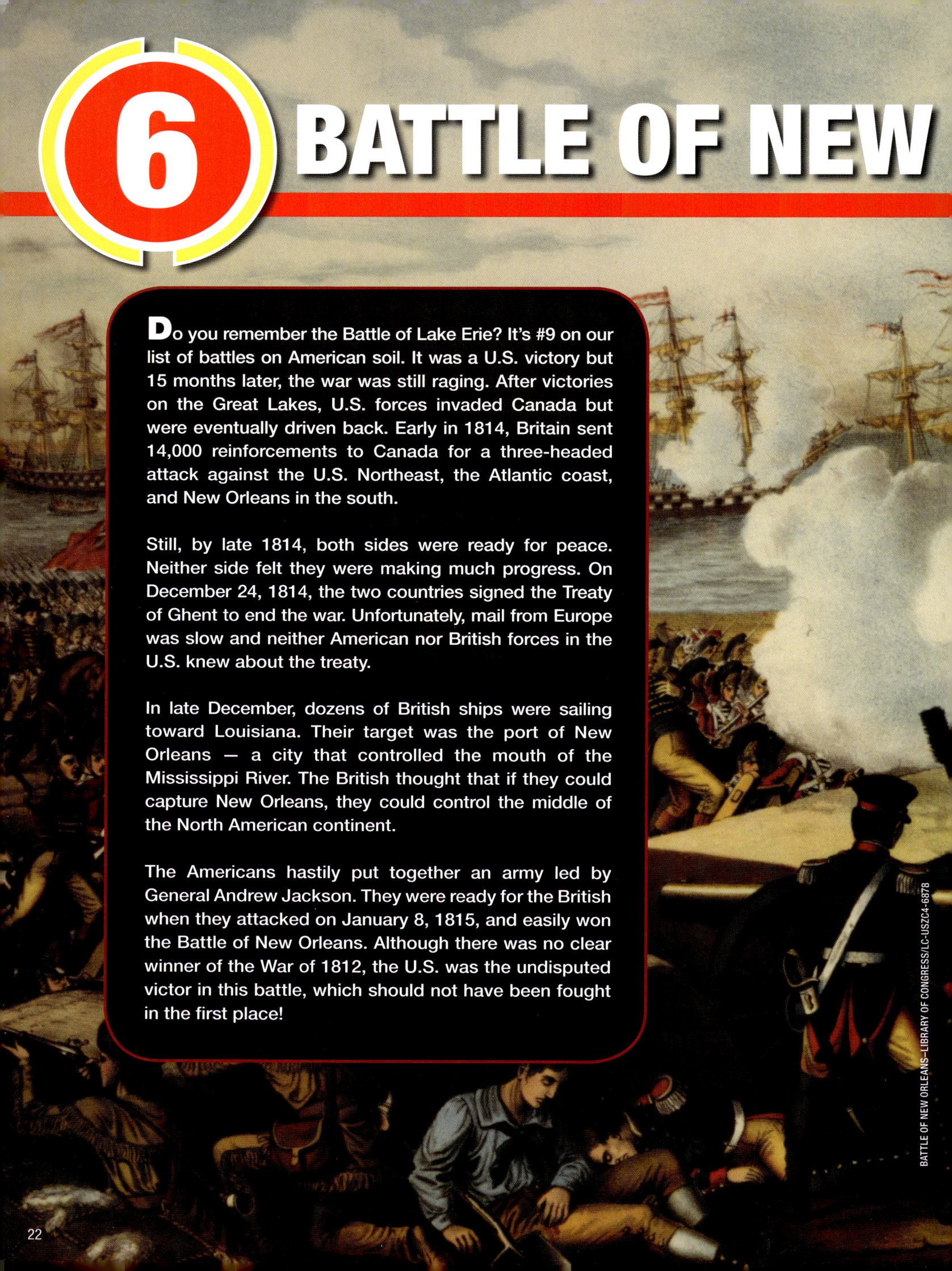

Do you remember the Battle of Lake Erie? It's #9 on our list of battles on American soil. It was a U.S. victory but 15 months later, the war was still raging. After victories on the Great Lakes, U.S. forces invaded Canada but were eventually driven back. Early in 1814, Britain sent 14,000 reinforcements to Canada for a three-headed attack against the U.S. Northeast, the Atlantic coast, and New Orleans in the south.

Still, by late 1814, both sides were ready for peace. Neither side felt they were making much progress. On December 24, 1814, the two countries signed the Treaty of Ghent to end the war. Unfortunately, mail from Europe was slow and neither American nor British forces in the U.S. knew about the treaty.

In late December, dozens of British ships were sailing toward Louisiana. Their target was the port of New Orleans — a city that controlled the mouth of the Mississippi River. The British thought that if they could capture New Orleans, they could control the middle of the North American continent.

The Americans hastily put together an army led by General Andrew Jackson. They were ready for the British when they attacked on January 8, 1815, and easily won the Battle of New Orleans. Although there was no clear winner of the War of 1812, the U.S. was the undisputed victor in this battle, which should not have been fought in the first place!

BATTLE OF NEW ORLEANS—LIBRARY OF CONGRESS/LC-USZC4-6878

ORLEANS

BOILING POINT: January 8, 1815

BATTLEGROUND: Banks of the Mississippi River — New Orleans, Louisiana

OPPOSING SIDES: U.S. army and various local militias versus British army

General Andrew Jackson commands American troops in battle against British soldiers on January 8, 1815, in this 1890 color print titled Battle of New Orleans.

BATTLE OF NEW ORLEANS

THE BATTLE BEGINS

British general Sir Edward Pakenham arrived in New Orleans with more than 7,500 men. General Andrew Jackson's force of 6,500 consisted of an unusual mix of Louisiana militia, Tennessee and Kentucky riflemen, Native Americans, free African Americans, and even a band of French pirates!

In late December, the British landed south of New Orleans and began attacking American forts. After several battles, Jackson chose to defend a position on the west bank of the Mississippi River known as Chalmette Plantation.

Quick Fact

As early as 1805, Britain and France, who were at war with one another, allowed only certain American ships to bring supplies to Europe. In response, Americans began to manufacture goods that they would normally buy from outside the country. As a result, manufacturing in the U.S. increased, and the Americans came to depend less on other countries for certain items, such as cotton goods.

? In what ways would the increase in U.S. manufacturing be a good thing?

Quick Fact

Jean Lafitte (La-feet) led the French pirates at the Battle of New Orleans. He has been called everything from "The Terror of the Gulf" to "Hero of New Orleans." Why did he and his fellow pirates help Jackson? Maybe they just wanted to protect New Orleans. The French Quarter in the city was where they sold their stolen goods.

THE TURNING POINT

On January 8, using heavy fog for cover, the British Redcoats attacked the Americans from the east. As they came close to the American lines, the fog lifted and they immediately came under heavy fire from American muskets and cannons. Within 30 minutes, the U.S. had won the battle. The British suffered as many as 2,000 casualties, including the death of three generals. Pakenham was one of the generals who was killed. The U.S. army suffered 71 casualties.

IN THE END

After the battle ended, word soon reached both British and U.S. forces that the Treaty of Ghent had been signed and the war was over. The British stopped interfering with U.S. shipping. Native Americans who had helped save Canada from an American invasion were now abandoned by Britain. After 1815, the U.S. government began moving the Native-American population to reservations across the Mississippi River.

Many Americans saw the War of 1812 as "the second war for independence" and patriotism soared. General Jackson was viewed as a national hero and later used his popularity to become president in 1829.

Redcoats: *British soldiers, known for their bright red uniforms*

The Expert Says...

" In that one glorious moment the nation had demonstrated that it had the strength, will, and ability to defend its freedom and prove to the world that it was here to stay. "

— Robert V. Rimimi, author of *The Battle of New Orleans: Andrew Jackson and America's First Military Victory*

A National Icon

General Andrew Jackson's leadership was a huge factor in the American victory at the Battle of New Orleans. Still, this was just one episode in an amazing career that led from the backwoods of Tennessee to the presidency. Take a look at this **profile** of Jackson's life.

BORN
March 15, 1767 in Waxhaw, South Carolina

REVOLUTIONARY WAR
At the age of 13, Jackson joined the Continental Army as a messenger. His older brother died in battle in 1779. Two years later, Jackson and his other brother were taken prisoner by British soldiers. They both caught smallpox, and his brother died soon after their release. Jackson's mother, who was a nurse for prisoners of war, became sick and died shortly after the death of her sons.

MILITARY LEADERSHIP
Jackson became commander of the Tennessee militia in 1802. Ten years later, he was given the rank of major general of U.S. forces. He became a national hero during the Battle of New Orleans.

PRESIDENTIAL ELECTION
Jackson was elected president in 1828. He received a lot of support from the West, which had not played a large part in American politics until Jackson's election. His image as "a common man" also won him support from Eastern farmers and city workers.

LEGACY
Jackson's legacy is mixed. For example, he championed the rights of farmers and industrial workers, and voting rights were expanded during his presidency. But Jackson also used the spoils system. And he had long favored the removal of Native Americans from their homes in the East. In 1830, the Indian Removable Act called for relocation, by force if necessary, of Native-American nations to Indian Territory, in what is today Oklahoma. In Florida, resistance to removal led to the Second Seminole War (1835-1842). Most of the Seminoles were killed or removed to Indian Territory.

spoils system: *practice of giving government jobs to political supporters*

? Find out more about the spoils system. Why would it be wrong to give government jobs to political supporters? Who should be hired for those jobs instead?

Take Note
The Battle of New Orleans was important for the young United States and deserves the #6 spot on our list. Even though it was fought after the War of 1812 was over, the battle was a decisive victory for the United States.
- News traveled very slowly in the 19th century. Imagine you had a chance to e-mail Andrew Jackson after the Treaty of Ghent. What would you say?

5 BATTLE OF LEXING

This engraving depicts a line of minutemen being fired upon by British troops in Lexington, Massachusetts.

TON AND CONCORD

BOILING POINT: April 19, 1775

BATTLEGROUND: Lexington and Concord, Massachusetts

OPPOSING SIDES: American colonists versus British soldiers

In the 1770s, many Americans were still loyal to Britain and King George III. But since the early 1760s, conflict had been growing between Britain and the American colonies over trade and taxes.

Between September 5 and October 26, 1774, delegates from 12 American colonies attended the First Continental Congress in Philadelphia. At this meeting, delegates voted to ban trade with the British until they lifted the so-called Intolerable Acts. These were laws passed to punish Massachusetts after the colonists staged the Boston Tea Party to protest the Tea Act. The delegates at the Congress also agreed to meet seven months later if the Intolerable Acts were not lifted. By that time, however, war with Britain had started.

Britain had responded with even more restrictions on American trade and had sent more troops to the colonies. A crackdown was ordered on Boston. On April 18, 1775, 700 British soldiers, led by General Thomas Gage, left Boston and marched toward Lexington and Concord to take possession of rebel supplies stored at Concord.

No one knows who fired the first shot at Lexington — the "shot heard 'round the world." But this was the first shot of the American Revolution.

Tea Act: law passed by Britain's parliament allowing the East India Company to sell tea directly to the colonies, harming local trade

? The phrase "shot heard 'round the world" has been used to describe many historical events. It comes from the *Concord Hymn* (1837), written by Ralph Waldo Emerson, and refers to the first shot at Lexington. What do you think it means?

BATTLE OF LEXINGTON AND CONCORD

THE BATTLE BEGINS

General Gage and his troops reached the town of Lexington at dawn on April 19. During the night, colonial spies reported seeing the British heading toward the town. Two messengers, Paul Revere and William Dawes, galloped toward Lexington, warning minutemen along the way. When the British marched into Lexington, they were met by about 70 minutemen under the command of Captain John Parker. A British officer ordered them to drop their weapons and leave the area. The revolutionaries refused and stood their ground.

minutemen: *members of the militia who pledged to fight at a minute's notice*

THE TURNING POINT

After just a few minutes of fighting, eight colonists lay dead. The minutemen fled while the British regrouped and marched to Concord, where they destroyed weapons and military supplies. As they started back to Boston, fighting broke out at a bridge north of the town. The British were forced to retreat. As they did so, hundreds of colonists fired at them from behind walls and trees. Only with the arrival of more troops from Boston were the British saved. The American colonists suffered fewer than 100 casualties, compared to Britain's 273.

IN THE END

British soldiers were trapped in Boston, surrounded by a huge army of American rebels. The Americans now knew that the tough British soldiers could be beaten. With the battle of Lexington and Concord, the Revolution had begun.

Quick Fact
British soldiers were known for the bright scarlet overcoats they wore. The American Continental Army later wore blue coats. But at Lexington and Concord, the men still wore their everyday clothes, even though paintings often depict them in blue.

A colored engraving, The Battle of Concord, shows the battle at the North Bridge.

The Expert Says...
"[P]oorly equipped, barely trained ... farmers and tradesmen had the audacity to challenge highly trained, tightly disciplined, well-supplied seasoned soldiers from the mightiest empire on Earth ..."

— Joseph L. Andrews, author of *The Sons of the American Revolution* Magazine

audacity: *boldness*

America's Forgotten Heroes

Check out the historical account below.

During the Revolutionary War, 20 percent of the population in the 13 colonies was African American. A few African Americans enjoyed freedom, but most were enslaved.

When the war began, many African Americans were barred from service for fear that they might not be loyal to the cause. However, as more and more soldiers died, recruiters found ways to include African Americans.

Most of the African-American soldiers were freedmen from the North. Some African Americans fought in integrated units while Rhode Island and Massachusettes had all-African-American regiments. The British offered freedom to enslaved African Americans who escaped, so long as they joined their ranks. Many enslaved African Americans gained their freedom this way.

The United States recognized many African-American soldiers for their part in the war. Salem Poor and Peter Salem were both praised for their bravery at the Battle of Bunker Hill. Austin Dabney of Georgia was given 112 acres of land for his role in several battles. Fifty years after the war, Edward Hector was given $50 (a lot of money at the time) for protecting an ammunition wagon when other soldiers ran away. James Armistead was commended by General Lafayette for his work as a spy.

integrated: *combined; mixed*
commended: *praised*

Peter Salem is crouched at right center in this 19th-century colored engraving of the Battle of Bunker Hill.

Take Note

The Battle of Lexington and Concord rides into the #5 spot. Although there wasn't a clear victory at Lexington and Concord, the American Revolution had clearly begun. People now had to choose sides and take up arms in defense of their political beliefs.
- Many Americans remained neutral at the start of the war. If you had been alive at that time, what group do you think you would have been a part of — patriots, Loyalists, or those who were neutral? Explain.

Loyalists: *American colonists who supported the British in the Revolutionary War*

4 BATTLE OF TR

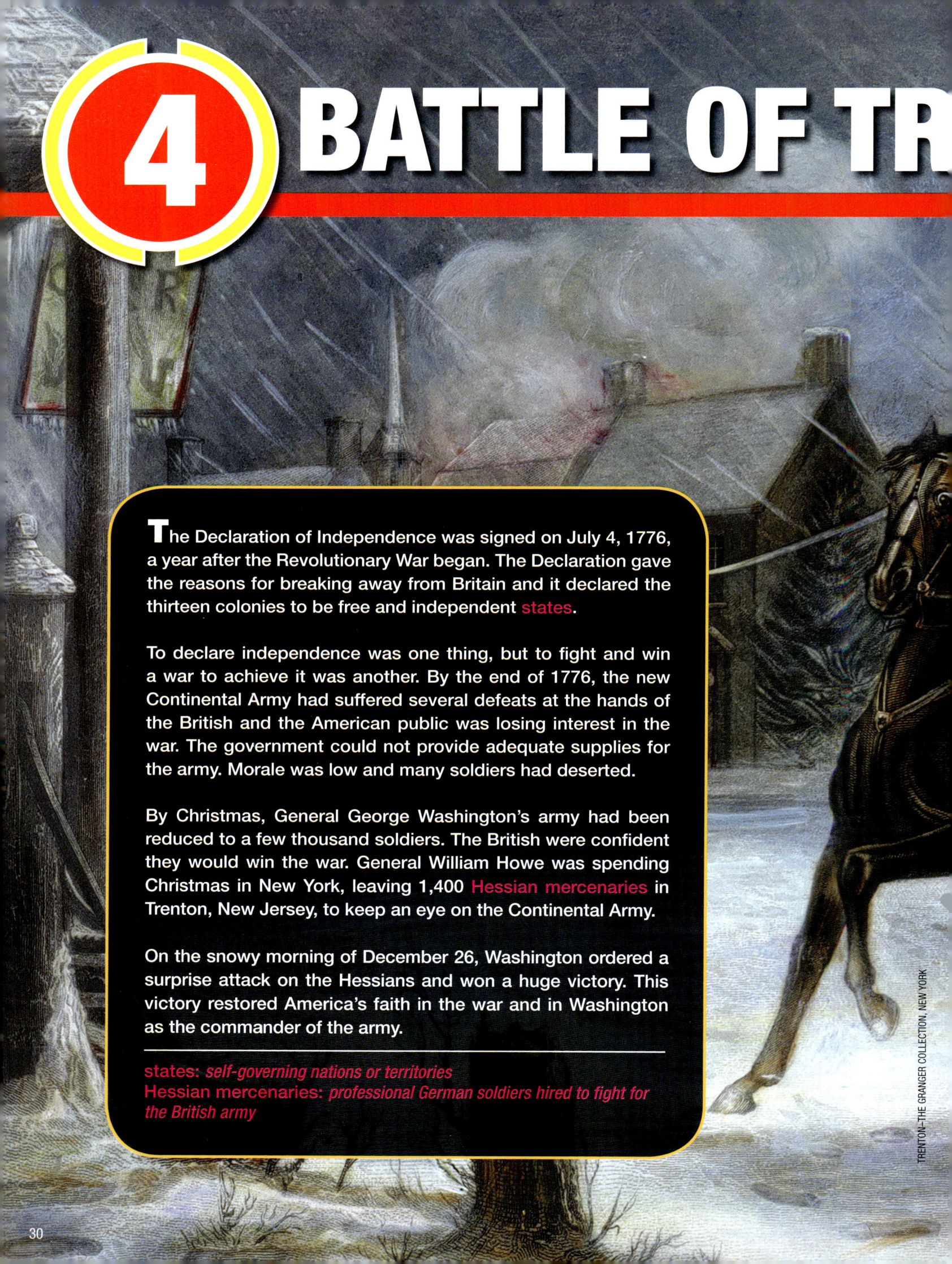

The Declaration of Independence was signed on July 4, 1776, a year after the Revolutionary War began. The Declaration gave the reasons for breaking away from Britain and it declared the thirteen colonies to be free and independent **states**.

To declare independence was one thing, but to fight and win a war to achieve it was another. By the end of 1776, the new Continental Army had suffered several defeats at the hands of the British and the American public was losing interest in the war. The government could not provide adequate supplies for the army. Morale was low and many soldiers had deserted.

By Christmas, General George Washington's army had been reduced to a few thousand soldiers. The British were confident they would win the war. General William Howe was spending Christmas in New York, leaving 1,400 **Hessian mercenaries** in Trenton, New Jersey, to keep an eye on the Continental Army.

On the snowy morning of December 26, Washington ordered a surprise attack on the Hessians and won a huge victory. This victory restored America's faith in the war and in Washington as the commander of the army.

---

states: *self-governing nations or territories*
Hessian mercenaries: *professional German soldiers hired to fight for the British army*

ENTON

BOILING POINT: December 26, 1776

BATTLEGROUND: Trenton, New Jersey, on the Delaware River

OPPOSING SIDES: American Continental Army versus Hessian mercenaries fighting for Britain

This 1876 steel engraving, Battle of Trenton, depicts General George Washington leading the early morning attack on Trenton, New Jersey.

BATTLE OF TRENTON

THE BATTLE BEGINS

The Hessians were under the command of Colonel Johann Rall. He assumed that Washington would not attack on Christmas because of the severe weather. But Washington had other ideas and attacked the Hessians on December 26. He knew that if they didn't win this battle, the Continental Army would most likely fall apart. On Christmas night in bitterly cold conditions, about 2,400 American soldiers rowed across the Delaware River, then hiked through the woods and fields to Trenton. They attacked at daybreak.

? How would you feel if you were part of an army that seemed overmatched?

Quick Fact

Most of Washington's soldiers had enlisted in the army for just one year, and their terms would be up on December 31. Washington was afraid that if he waited until the spring to attack the British, he would have few soldiers left.

THE TURNING POINT

The Hessians, still recovering from their Christmas celebrations, had just a small guard posted. Washington's arrival caused panic, and they soon surrendered. More than 100 Hessians were killed or wounded and as many as 900 taken prisoner. Others escaped to the forest. American casualties were few. Four or five American soldiers were wounded and it is believed that two or three soldiers froze to death during the march to Trenton.

IN THE END

Washington was able to win another victory over the British a few days later in Princeton, New Jersey. The two victories were celebrated in the newspapers, and new recruits rushed to join the army. Faith in Washington as a general was restored. The British, who thought the war would soon be over, realized that the Americans were not backing down.

In 1851, artist Emanuel Gottlieb Leutze painted George Washington Crossing the Delaware.

The Expert Says...

"Trenton was little short of spectacular. It did nothing less than keep the American cause alive …"

— James L. Stokesbury, author of *A Short History of the American Revolution*

WOMEN IN THE REVOLUTION

Molly Hays McCauley

Women played a large role during the Revolutionary War. Some women nursed injured soldiers. Some were spies who collected vital information. Others dressed up as men and fought in battle. Below are profiles of four women who played major roles in the war.

ELIZABETH BURGIN

Burgin often visited American prisoners on British ships in New York Harbor, bringing them food and lifting their spirits. One day, she was approached by an American officer who asked her to help him free the prisoners. Burgin alerted the prisoners to the planned escape. Over 200 escaped with her help. In 1781, Burgin was awarded a pension for her service to the soldiers in the war.

MOLLY HAYS McCAULEY

McCauley, also known as "Molly Pitcher," followed her husband into battle, bringing troops food and pitchers of water. At the Battle of Valley Forge, McCauley saw her husband get shot in the arm. She rushed over to her husband's cannon and fired several rounds at the British troops. Her action caught the attention of General Washington, and he nicknamed her "Sergeant Molly Pitcher."

DEBORAH SAMPSON

Sampson (or Samson) enlisted in the Continental Army in 1782. At that time, women weren't allowed to enlist, but that didn't stop her. She cut her hair, dressed as a man, and changed her name to Robert Shurtleff. Her secret was discovered when she caught a fever in 1783 and was sent to a hospital. At the end of the war, Sampson was given an honorable discharge.

CATHERINE MOORE BARRY

Barry lived in South Carolina, where the British were marching against the American forces of General Morgan. Morgan asked Barry to ride to every town she could and rally colonists who supported the revolution. Barry gathered a group of soldiers to join Morgan's troops. Morgan laid a trap for the British and forced them to retreat.

> **?** What qualities do you think these women shared? Think of some of the challenges they faced as they tried to do their bit for the nation.

Quick Fact
Some historians suggest that "Molly Pitcher" was a nickname given to many different women who carried water to troops on the battlefield — not just to Molly Hays McCauley.

Take Note

The Battle of Trenton comes in at #4 on our list. Although Trenton was a small battle in the Revolutionary War, it was a crucial one for the struggling Continental Army. Without that victory, the army might have faded away, and with it, American independence.

- American soldiers were fighting against mercenaries paid by Britain. Do you think this helped the Americans win the Battle of Trenton? Explain.

3 BATTLE OF PE

Just before 8:00 A.M. on December 7, 1941, the message *"Tora! Tora! Tora!"* (Tiger! Tiger! Tiger!) was radioed to Japanese ships approaching Hawaii. Commander Mitsuo Fuchida, who led the first air attack on Pearl Harbor, was letting the ships know that the surprise attack was successful. Within minutes, hundreds of Japanese warplanes were dropping bombs over Pearl Harbor and setting ships ablaze. For the first time since the War of 1812, a foreign nation had attacked U.S. forces on American soil.

Japan had been expanding its military in the years before the attack on Pearl Harbor. In 1931, Japan invaded Manchuria, a province in northern China that was rich in natural resources. In July, 1937, Japanese forces began their attacks on Chinese cities, occupying Shanghai and Nanking. Over the next few years, they conducted massive air bombardments on every city in China. Japan was determined to become a powerful empire that would rule Asia and the Pacific Ocean. Now they were hoping to cripple the U.S. Navy at Pearl Harbor.

The Japanese damaged a number of battleships and destroyed many American warplanes. And while American forces fought back, they were totally unprepared for the attack. Most of the Japanese planes escaped with little damage. However, the Japanese failed in their goal — to completely eliminate the U.S. Pacific Fleet.

Within 24 hours of the attack, the U.S. declared war on Japan.

U.S. Pacific Fleet: *branch of the U.S. Navy based at Pearl Harbor and on duty in the Pacific Ocean*

ARL HARBOR

BOILING POINT: December 7, 1941

BATTLEGROUND: Pearl Harbor, Hawaii

OPPOSING SIDES: Imperial Japanese Navy versus United States Pacific Fleet

Pearl Harbor, Hawaii: A small boat rescues a seaman while the 31,800-ton USS West Virginia *burns in the harbor.*

BATTLE OF PEARL HARBOR

THE BATTLE BEGINS

Two aerial attacks were launched from six Japanese aircraft carriers. Their 360 bombers and fighter planes inflicted heavy damage almost immediately. The American aircraft carriers the Japanese hoped to destroy were away at sea, but there were eight huge battleships in the harbor, along with smaller ships. U.S. planes were parked wing-to-wing and were easy targets for the Japanese fighters.

> **?** Why do you think the Japanese attacked on a Sunday morning?

THE TURNING POINT

The U.S. was completely unprepared for the attack. Had more than just a few U.S. aircraft survived the attacks on their airfields, they could have drawn fire away from the ships. As it was, the warships were also easy targets. The crew of the USS *Pennsylvania*, which was in dry dock, responded quickly and their anti-aircraft gunners were able to drive off most of the attacking planes and save the ship. But eight battleships and 10 other naval vessels were destroyed or heavily damaged. One, the USS *Arizona*, was sent to the bottom of the sea with more than 1,000 of its crew. Almost 200 planes were destroyed and Pearl Harbor lay in ruins.

---

dry dock: area where ships are repaired; the dock is flooded to let ships in and then drained so work can begin

Quick Fact
A U.S. Army private noticed the incoming Japanese planes on the radar but was told they were probably the B-17 planes that were expected to come from the U.S. at that time.

> **?** Do some research. Find out how radar has changed since the days of World War II. Do you think this attack could happen again? Explain your answer.

IN THE END

More than 2,400 Americans were killed and almost 1,200 wounded in this attack. The Pacific Fleet was crippled but not destroyed. The three aircraft carriers at sea escaped attack, and two of the damaged ships were later repaired. On December 8, the U.S. declared war on Japan. Within months, the U.S. Navy struck back, soundly beating the Japanese at the Battle of Midway. Four years later, Japan surrendered after the nuclear attacks on the cities of Hiroshima and Nagasaki.

Quick Fact
In June 1942, the U.S. Navy defeated the Imperial Japanese Navy at the Battle of Midway. The U.S. destroyed four Japanese aircraft carriers and seriously weakened the Japanese navy. After the battle, the U.S. set up a submarine base on Midway, allowing for deeper strikes into Japanese waters.

The Expert Says...

" Although Pearl Harbor started the Pacific War, a war that Japan would lose badly, the attack itself was no failure. The Japanese wanted to cripple the Pacific Fleet and give them the space to invade Southeast Asia. They did. "

— Bruce Robinson, author of *Pearl Harbor: A Rude Awakening*

Firefighters after the attack on Pearl Harbor

A Date Which Will Live in Infamy

President Franklin Delano Roosevelt's Pearl Harbor Address to the Nation
December 8, 1941

Yesterday, December 7th, 1941 — a date which will live in infamy — the United States of America was suddenly and deliberately attacked by naval and air forces of the Empire of Japan.

The United States was at peace with that nation and … was still in conversation with its government and its emperor looking toward the maintenance of peace in the Pacific. …

It will be recorded that the distance of Hawaii from Japan makes it obvious that the attack was deliberately planned many days or even weeks ago. During the intervening time, the Japanese government has deliberately sought to deceive the United States by false statements and expressions of hope for continued peace.

I believe that I interpret the will of the Congress and of the people when I assert that we will not only defend ourselves to the uttermost, but will make it very certain that this form of treachery shall never again endanger us.

Hostilities exist. There is no blinking at the fact that our people, our territory, and our interests are in grave danger.

With confidence in our armed forces, with the unbounding determination of our people, we will gain the inevitable triumph …

---

infamy: *reputation for something shocking and brutal*
intervening: *occurring between events*
treachery: *betrayal*
unbounding: *limitless*

? Choose one sentence from Roosevelt's speech that stands out for you. Explain why you chose this sentence.

Take Note

The attack on Pearl Harbor comes in at #3 on our list. It was a decisive victory for Japan, but one that would be reversed in the years to come. The Battle of Trenton was a great victory for the U.S., but it did not affect any other country except Britain. The attack on Pearl Harbor brought the U.S. into World War II and changed world history.
- Compare this surprise attack with Washington's attack at the Battle of Trenton. Which was the more successful? Why?

5   4   **3**   2   1

② BATTLE OF YO

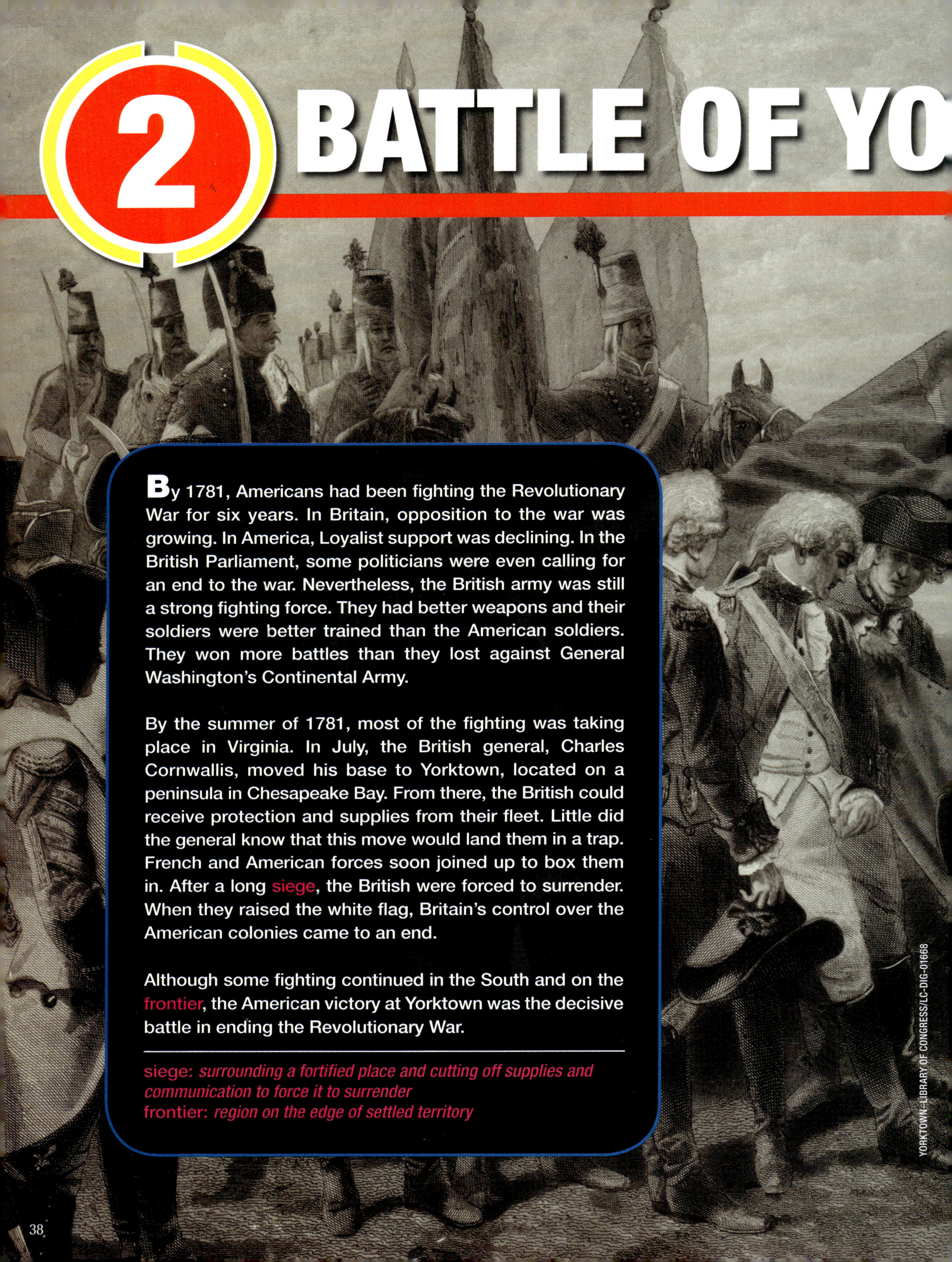

By 1781, Americans had been fighting the Revolutionary War for six years. In Britain, opposition to the war was growing. In America, Loyalist support was declining. In the British Parliament, some politicians were even calling for an end to the war. Nevertheless, the British army was still a strong fighting force. They had better weapons and their soldiers were better trained than the American soldiers. They won more battles than they lost against General Washington's Continental Army.

By the summer of 1781, most of the fighting was taking place in Virginia. In July, the British general, Charles Cornwallis, moved his base to Yorktown, located on a peninsula in Chesapeake Bay. From there, the British could receive protection and supplies from their fleet. Little did the general know that this move would land them in a trap. French and American forces soon joined up to box them in. After a long siege, the British were forced to surrender. When they raised the white flag, Britain's control over the American colonies came to an end.

Although some fighting continued in the South and on the frontier, the American victory at Yorktown was the decisive battle in ending the Revolutionary War.

---

siege: *surrounding a fortified place and cutting off supplies and communication to force it to surrender*
frontier: *region on the edge of settled territory*

RKTOWN

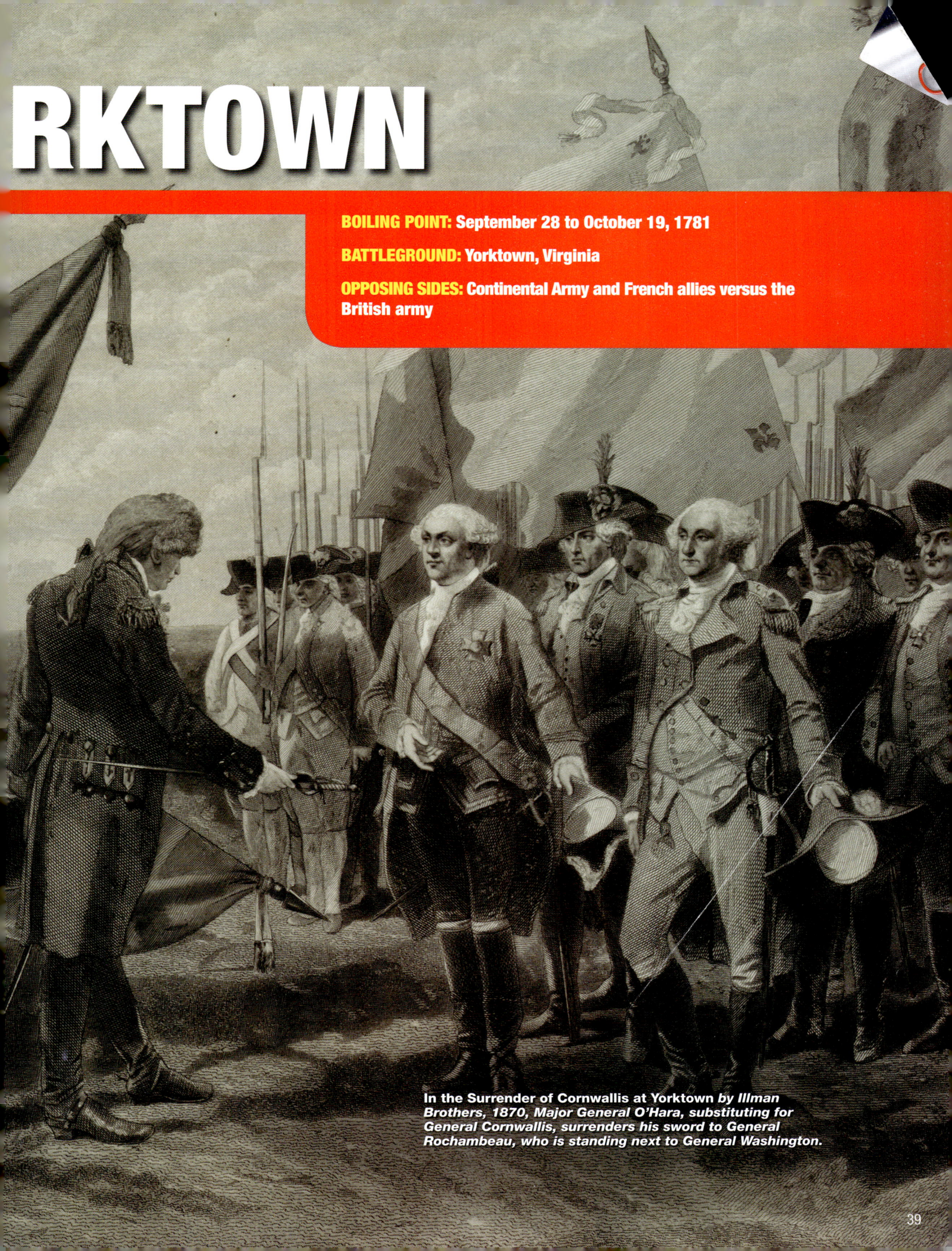

BOILING POINT: September 28 to October 19, 1781

BATTLEGROUND: Yorktown, Virginia

OPPOSING SIDES: Continental Army and French allies versus the British army

In the Surrender of Cornwallis at Yorktown *by Illman Brothers*, 1870, Major General O'Hara, substituting for General Cornwallis, surrenders his sword to General Rochambeau, who is standing next to General Washington.

BATTLE OF YORKTOWN

THE BATTLE BEGINS

When General Cornwallis moved his forces to Yorktown, a small American force led by generals Lafayette, von Steuben, and Anthony Wayne kept watch on the British but did not attack. In late August 1781, General Washington learned that he would have help against the British. A large French fleet from the West Indies was sailing north to block Chesapeake Bay. Meanwhile, Washington began to move his troops south. French soldiers under General Rochambeau (Raw-shahn-boh) joined Washington's army.

On September 5, the British navy was defeated by the French and was forced to return to New York for repairs and supplies. The British forces at Yorktown were alone, and were soon blocked in — on the coast by the French fleet and on land by the Americans and their French allies.

Quick Fact
When the British marched out of Yorktown to surrender on October 19, their band played a song called "The World Turned Upside Down," recognizing the surprising American victory.

? Why was the American victory such a surprise?

Surrender of Cornwallis at Yorktown, a print published by N. Currier

THE TURNING POINT

Washington and Rochambeau arrived in Yorktown on September 28 and the siege of the town began. By October 14, the French and Americans had captured two British forts. The British navy's attempts to break the French blockade failed. The Americans and French continued to bombard Yorktown with cannon fire, turning the town to rubble. On October 17, Cornwallis realized he had no chance and requested a truce. Two days later, he surrendered to Washington.

Quick Fact
Five days after Cornwallis surrendered at Yorktown, 7,000 more British troops finally arrived at Chesapeake Bay. Upon hearing of the surrender, they turned back.

? What do you think would have happened if the 7,000 British troops had managed to get to Cornwallis earlier?

IN THE END

Even though there were a lot of British soldiers left in America, and a few more small battles were fought, the Battle of Yorktown really settled the war. When news of Cornwallis's surrender reached Britain, its government decided to ask for peace. In September 1783, Britain and America signed the Treaty of Paris, which granted the United States independence.

The Expert Says...
> Though the British still had 26,000 troops in North America after Yorktown, their resolve to win the war was nothing like it had been before Yorktown.

— Sandy Groves, author of *History of the Siege of Yorktown*

resolve: *determination*

Flags of the Revolution

Battle flags were very important to soldiers in the Revolutionary War. Commanders used the flags to tell their troops apart from the enemy. Fighting units used them so they could stay together on the battlefield. It was considered an honor to carry a flag into battle, and brave men would fight to the death to keep it out of enemy hands. Take a look at the various flags of the American Revolution in the pictorial essay below.

This white flag with a pine tree was flown at sea by American ships. It was meant to represent the Liberty Tree in Boston. Soldiers from New England also carried this flag. Variations of the flag sometimes bore the inscription, "An Appeal to Heaven."

DON'T TREAD ON ME

A yellow flag carried by the South Carolina Navy featured a coiled rattlesnake and the motto "Don't Tread On Me." The snake represented Americans' attitude toward the British — step on us, and we'll bite back!

tread: trample

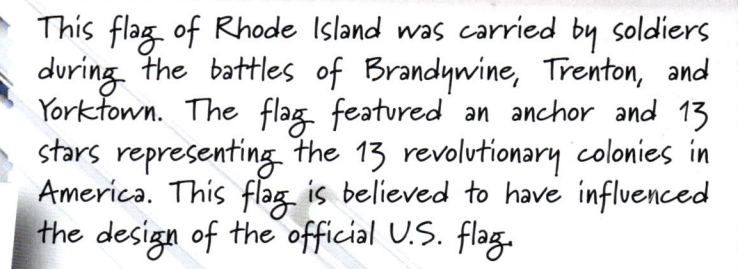

This flag of Rhode Island was carried by soldiers during the battles of Brandywine, Trenton, and Yorktown. The flag featured an anchor and 13 stars representing the 13 revolutionary colonies in America. This flag is believed to have influenced the design of the official U.S. flag.

On June 14, 1777, this flag became the official flag of the United States. The first flag bore 13 stars representing the 13 states in the Union, but this number would change many times over the next 200 years.

Take Note

The Battle of Yorktown is the second most decisive battle on our list because it effectively ended the Revolutionary War and established American independence.
- The Americans won the Revolutionary War against British forces who ranked among the best in the world. Why do you think they were successful?

2   **1**

1 BATTLE OF

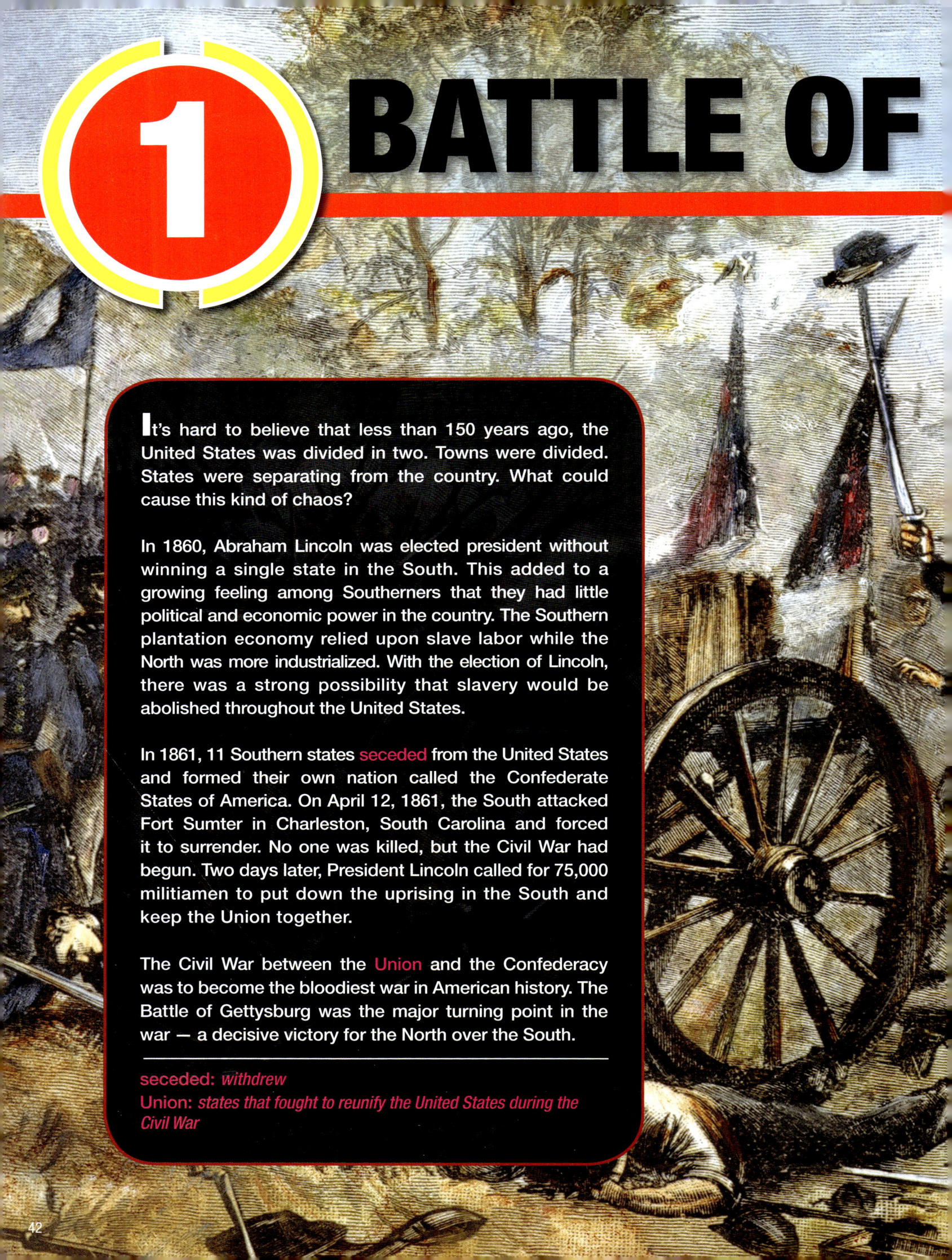

It's hard to believe that less than 150 years ago, the United States was divided in two. Towns were divided. States were separating from the country. What could cause this kind of chaos?

In 1860, Abraham Lincoln was elected president without winning a single state in the South. This added to a growing feeling among Southerners that they had little political and economic power in the country. The Southern plantation economy relied upon slave labor while the North was more industrialized. With the election of Lincoln, there was a strong possibility that slavery would be abolished throughout the United States.

In 1861, 11 Southern states seceded from the United States and formed their own nation called the Confederate States of America. On April 12, 1861, the South attacked Fort Sumter in Charleston, South Carolina and forced it to surrender. No one was killed, but the Civil War had begun. Two days later, President Lincoln called for 75,000 militiamen to put down the uprising in the South and keep the Union together.

The Civil War between the Union and the Confederacy was to become the bloodiest war in American history. The Battle of Gettysburg was the major turning point in the war — a decisive victory for the North over the South.

seceded: *withdrew*
Union: *states that fought to reunify the United States during the Civil War*

GETTYSBURG

BOILING POINT: July 1–3, 1863

BATTLEGROUND: Gettysburg, Pennsylvania

OPPOSING SIDES: Confederate army versus Union army

Pickett's Charge, a wood engraving from a drawing by A.R. Waud — Lewis A. Armistead, shown here with his hat on his sword, was one of three brigade commanders killed during the charge.

BATTLE OF GETTYSBURG

THE BATTLE BEGINS

During the first two years of the Civil War, the Confederate general, Robert E. Lee, had won victories against Union forces, although he had lost at Antietam when he first invaded the North. In June 1861, Lee invaded the North for a second time, crossing into southern Pennsylvania. He hoped that a Confederate victory here would force the Union to end the war. He also thought it might lead to European recognition and aid for the Confederacy.

When the Confederate soldiers approached Gettysburg, neither side had planned for a battle. The Confederates didn't know the town was already occupied by Union soldiers, led by General George Meade. On July 1, the fighting began. By the end of the day, the Confederates had pushed the Union line back to Cemetery Ridge, just south of the town.

THE TURNING POINT

After two days of fighting, Lee decided to gamble everything on one massive charge. On July 3, more than 13,000 Confederate soldiers, led by General George Pickett, charged across an open field toward Cemetery Ridge in what became known as Pickett's Charge. The Confederates marched right into a hail of bullets and cannon balls. By the time the Confederates finally retreated, 28,000 of their troops were dead or wounded. The North suffered 23,000 casualties.

General George Meade at the Battle of Gettysburg, July 3, 1863

IN THE END

With one-third of their army dead or wounded, the Confederates began to march back to Virginia. Meade did not pursue Lee's troops, allowing them to get away.

The victory at Gettysburg built Union confidence and ended Confederate hopes for a victory in the North. Although the Civil War would continue for two more years, the Battle of Gettysburg put the South on the defensive.

Quick Fact
The Civil War ended after General Lee surrendered to Ulysses S. Grant on April 9, 1865. The war was the most costly in U.S. history. More than 600,000 people died and the Southern states were left in ruins.

The Expert Says...
" Gettysburg marked the turning point of the war. The Confederates never regained the initiative. "

— Richard Holmes, author of *Battlefield: Decisive Conflicts In History*

initiative: *ability to choose the direction of the war*

A Letter From Lincoln

General Meade's victory over General Lee's army was celebrated across the North. But there was one person who wasn't satisfied with how the battle ended — President Lincoln. He wrote a letter to Meade explaining how disappointed he was that the general did not pursue Lee's army after the victory.

Executive Mansion, Washington, July 14, 1863

Major General Meade,

... I am very very grateful to you for the magnificent success you gave the cause of the country at Gettysburg; ... You fought and beat the enemy at Gettysburg ... He retreated; and you did not, as it seemed to me, pressingly pursue him; ... You had at least twenty thousand veteran troops directly with you, and as many more raw ones within supporting distance, all in addition to those who fought with you at Gettysburg; ...

I do not believe you appreciate the magnitude of the misfortune involved in Lee's escape. He was within your easy grasp, and to have closed upon him would, in connection with our other late successes, have ended the war. As it is, the war will be prolonged indefinitely. If you could not safely attack Lee last Monday, how can you possibly do so South of the river, when you can take with you very few more than two thirds of the force you then had in hand? ... Your golden opportunity is gone, and I am distressed immeasurably because of it.

I beg you will not consider this a prosecution ... of yourself. As you had learned that I was dissatisfied, I have thought it best to kindly tell you why.

Abraham Lincoln

magnitude: *significance; importance*
indefinitely: *for an unknown amount of time*
prosecution: *accusation; charge*

? What words does Lincoln use in his letter to emphasize his disappointment?

Quick Fact
In November 1863, President Lincoln gave his memorable Gettysburg Address during a dedication ceremony on the battlefield. His two-minute speech was a tribute to the soldiers who died there and to the ideals that they were fighting for — liberty, equality, and democracy.

Take Note
The Battle of Gettysburg secures the #1 spot on our list of decisive battles on U.S. soil. This battle was a clear victory for the Union, although both sides suffered enormous casualties. Gettysburg was the major turning point of the Civil War. Union armies would go on to win victories in the West and in the South, finally bringing an end to the war two years after Gettysburg.
• What might have happened if Meade had pursued Lee's army? Do you think the war would have been over sooner? Explain.

We Thought …

Here are the criteria we used in ranking the 10 most decisive battles on American soil.

The battle:
- Had a lasting impact on the future of the United States
- Changed the direction or outcome of a war
- Proved that the U.S. had a strong military
- Led to the creation of the United States or added more states to the nation
- Showed that miliary leadership was a major factor in winning
- Helped win rights and freedom

46